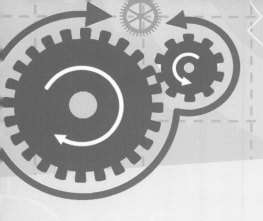

Get to Know Levers

by Karen Volpe

Crabtree Publishing Company

www.crabtreebooks.com

Crabtree Publishing Company

www.crabtreebooks.com

Author: Karen Volpe
Editors: Molly Aloian, Reagan Miller, Crystal Sikkens
Project coordinator: Robert Walker
Prepress technicians: Ken Wright, Margaret Amy Salter
Production coordinator: Margaret Amy Salter
Cover design: Samara Parent
Coordinating editor: Chester Fisher
Series and project editor: Penny Dowdy
Project manager: Kumar Kunal (Q2AMEDIA)
Art direction: Dibakar Acharjee (Q2AMEDIA)
Design: Ritu Chopra (Q2AMEDIA)
Photo research: Farheen Aadil (Q2AMEDIA)

Photographs:
Greg Fiume/NewSport/Corbis: p. 24
Marc Crabtree: p. 20
Ingram photo objects: p. 4 (lever), 31
Istockphoto: Rich Legg: cover; Clayton Hansen:
    p. 4 (wheel and axle); Peter Austin: p. 9;
    Jennifer Daley: p. 13; Kate Leigh: p. 28
Shutterstock: Medvedev Andrey: p. 4 (screw);
    Andrjuss: p. 4 (wedge); Julián Rovagnati:
    p. 4 (inclined plane); Harley Molesworth:
    p. 4 (pulley); Duard van der Westhuizen: p. 5;
    Monkey Business Images: p. 16; Jaimie Duplass:
    p. 17; Jules Studio: p. 21; Sonya Etchison: p. 25;
    Stanislav Komogorov: p. 29

Illustrations:
Q2AMedia Art Bank: p. 6, 7, 10, 11, 14, 15, 18, 19,
    22, 23, 26, 27

Library and Archives Canada Cataloguing in Publication

Volpe, Karen
    Get to know levers / Karen Volpe.

(Get to know simple machines)
Includes index.
ISBN 978-0-7787-4467-2 (bound).--ISBN 978-0-7787-4484-9 (pbk.)

    1. Levers--Juvenile literature.
I. Title. II. Series: Get to know simple machines

TL147.V64 2009   j621.8   C2009-900794-0

Library of Congress Cataloging-in-Publication Data

Volpe, Karen.
    Get to know levers / Karen Volpe.
        p. cm. -- (Get to know simple machines)
    Includes index.
    ISBN 978-0-7787-4484-9 (pbk. : alk. paper) -- ISBN 978-0-7787-4467-2
(reinforced library binding : alk. paper)
    1. Levers--Juvenile literature. I. Title. II. Series.

TJ147.V67 2009
621.8--dc22
                                              2009004583

Crabtree Publishing Company

www.crabtreebooks.com   1-800-387-7650

Published in Canada
Crabtree Publishing
616 Welland Ave.
St. Catharines, ON
L2M 5V6

Published in the United States
Crabtree Publishing
PMB16A
350 Fifth Ave., Suite 3308
New York, NY 10118

Published in the United Kingdom
Crabtree Publishing
White Cross Mills
High Town, Lancaster
LA1 4XS

Published in Australia
Crabtree Publishing
386 Mt. Alexander Rd.
Ascot Vale (Melbourne)
VIC 3032

Contents

What is a Simple Machine?

All people have jobs to do. Some jobs take a lot of **energy**. Energy is the ability to do **work**. Simple machines help people get jobs done without working too hard. This is called **mechanical advantage**.

Simple machines are tools that are made up of very few parts. There are six kinds of simple machines. They are inclined planes, **levers**, pulleys, wedges, screws, and wheels and axles.

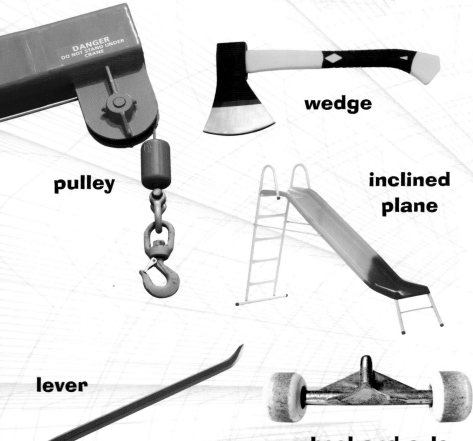

pulley

wedge

inclined plane

lever

wheel and axle

screw

These pictures show an example of each kind of simple machine.

4

One kind of simple machine is a lever. A lever is a bar that rests on a turning point. Levers are used to lift or move objects.

Seesaws, hammers, and wheelbarrows are examples of levers you may see everyday.

The tab on this soda can is a lever, too. The tab is used to open the can.

How Levers Make Work Easier

Let's explore how using a lever makes work easier. You will need:

2 pencils   **books**

Step 1

Place the stack of books on the table. Put your thumb under the edge of the stack. Try lifting the stack using only your thumb. Can you do it?

Step 2

Now place the tip of one pencil under the edge of the bottom book in the stack.

Place the second pencil under the first pencil, so the pencils make a +. Make sure the bottom pencil is close to the edge of the book stack.

Now push down on the top pencil using your thumb. Were you able to lift the books? The pencils act as a lever.

Parts of a Lever

To make a lever, you need a board or bar. The bar rests on a turning point called a **fulcrum**. The fulcrum allows you to push down on one end of the bar to raise the other end of the bar. This is called the **effort**. A lever can be used to lift or move an object. The object being moved is called the **load**.

Effort

Load

Fulcrum

effort

The load is the nail. The effort is the pulling hand. The fulcrum is the hammer head.

load

fulcrum

Catapult Shooter

Levers can also be used as a catapult. You will need:

craft stick   **pencil**   **mini marshmallows**   **small cup**

Get down on the floor. Place the craft stick across the pencil. The pencil is your fulcrum. Place a marshmallow on the end of the craft stick touching the floor.

Tap the empty end of the craft stick to flip the marshmallow in the air.

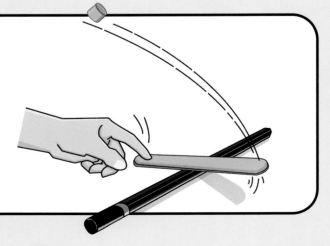

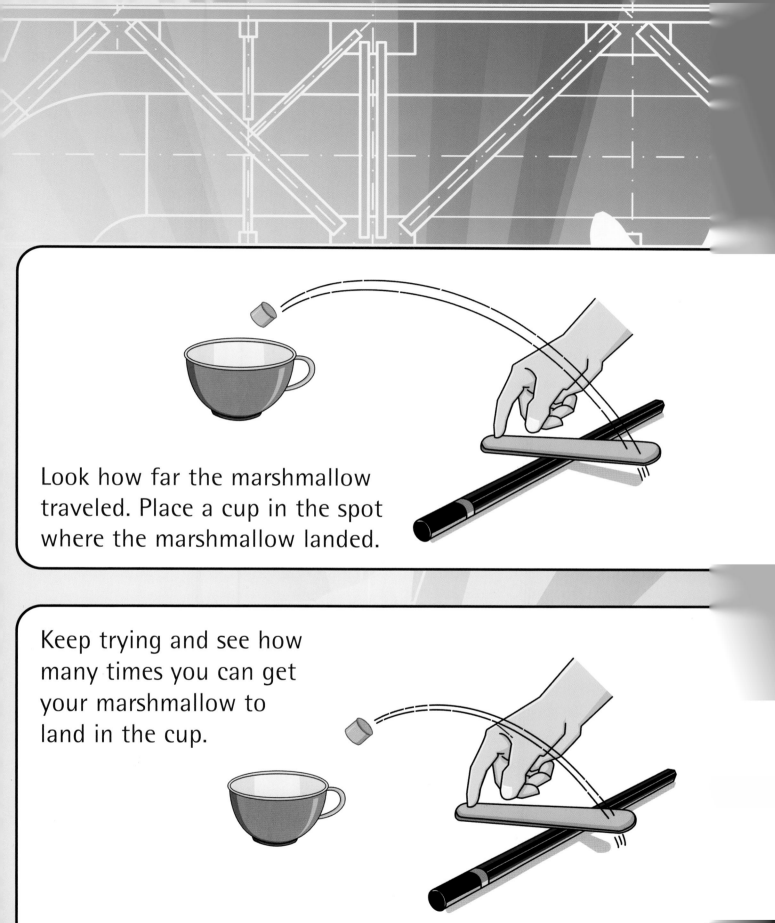

Look how far the marshmallow traveled. Place a cup in the spot where the marshmallow landed.

Keep trying and see how many times you can get your marshmallow to land in the cup.

First-Class Levers

There are three different kinds of levers. Each one helps you do different things. A **first-class lever** helps you move heavy objects. It has the fulcrum between the load and effort.

You can move the load by pushing down or pulling up on one end. The closer the fulcrum is to the load, the less effort you will need to lift the load.

First-Class Lever

Effort

Load

Fulcrum

Did you know that a seesaw is a first-class lever? Can you spot the seesaw's fulcrum?

Moving the Fulcrum

Let's see how moving the fulcrum in a first-class lever changes the effort needed to move a load. You will need:

pennies   **pencil**

ruler

Step 1

Place the ruler over the pencil at the six-inch (15-cm) mark. The pencil is the fulcrum. Put two pennies at the one-inch (2.5-cm) mark. This is your load.

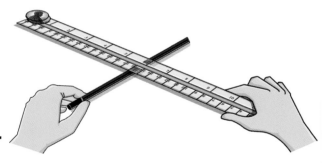

Step 2

Add pennies to the 12-inch (30-cm) mark, one at a time. How many pennies did you add to lift the load?

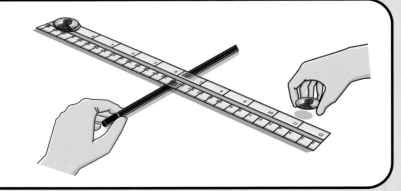

14

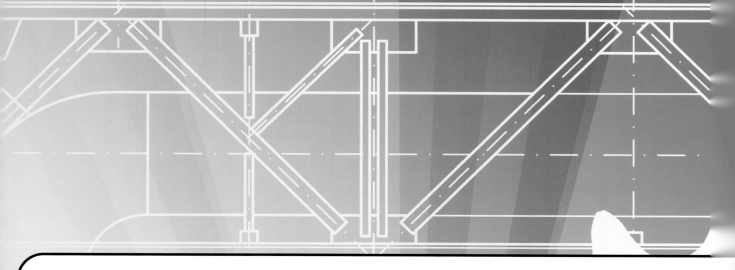

Now move the pencil to the eight-inch (20-cm) mark on the ruler. Add pennies until the load is lifted. How many pennies did you need to lift the load?

Try moving the pencil to the five-inch (12-cm) mark. How many pennies do you need to lift the two-penny load?

Second-Class Levers

Another kind of lever is the **second-class lever**. In a second-class lever, the load is between the fulcrum and the effort. Examples of second-class levers include wheelbarrows, bottle openers, nutcrackers, and wrenches.

The fulcrum is the wheel. The girl is the load. The boy is the effort.

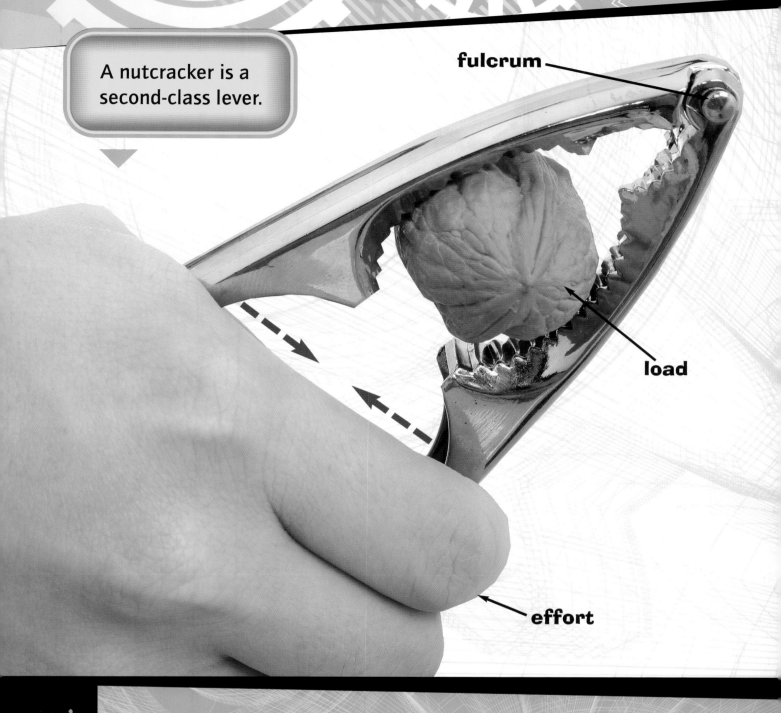

A nutcracker is a second-class lever.

fulcrum

load

effort

Can you crack a nut with just your bare hands? Probably not! Levers can help you crack even the toughest nut! What other second-class levers can you think of?

Crack that Nut

Investigate how second-class levers make work easier by using a nutcracker and different size nuts. You will need:

nuts   **nutcracker**

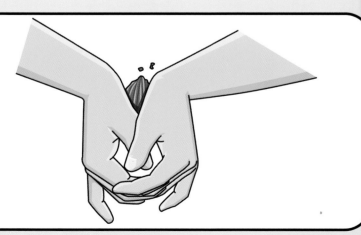

Collect a few nuts of different shapes and sizes.

Try to crack the nuts using only your hands.

18

Now use the
nutcracker.
Squeeze the
nutcracker with
your hands. Can
you crack the nut?

Try cracking different size
nuts. Are some easier than
others? Can you crack any
nuts without using a
nutcracker?

Third-Class Levers

A **third-class lever** has the same parts as all other levers. In a third-class lever, the effort is between the load and fulcrum. A third-class lever moves a load a long distance with a small effort.

Examples of third-class levers include a fishing rod, a shovel, a broom, and tongs.

A fishing rod has the load at the end of the line. The effort is your hands holding the rod. The fulcrum is your wrist.

Your shoulders act as the fulcrum in tennis.

Small Effort, Big Result

Explore how a third-class lever can produce a big result with only a small effort. You will need:

ball

bottle caps

paper clip

kitchen tongs

safety pin

eraser

tweezers

Arrange your items on a flat surface.

Use your tongs to pick up the items one at a time. Observe how far the tongs move where you squeeze. Do you notice how far the tongs move at the grabbing end?

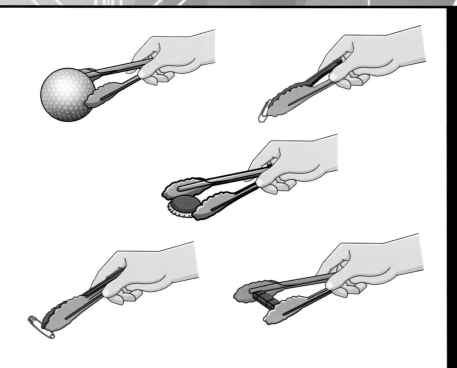

Step 2

Now try using your tweezers to pick up some of the smaller items. Compare how far the tweezers move on the squeezing end with the grabbing end. Which end moves a greater distance?

Step 3

Levers for Fun

Levers help us have fun! Many of the activities we enjoy use levers. Scooping sand for a sand castle is a third-class lever. The sand is the load. Your hand is the effort. Your bending elbow is the fulcrum.

Many sports, such as hockey, tennis, baseball, and golf, use third-class levers.

Can you think of another activity that uses a lever like this baseball bat?

A third-class lever makes that big hit possible. Your arms supply the effort. The fulcrum is your shoulder and the load is the ball. Home run!

All Around You

When you go to the beach you can see many levers in action. Can you find some examples of levers? Can you identify the load, fulcrum, and effort?

Effort: Hand
Fulcrum: Wrist or elbow
Load: Sand

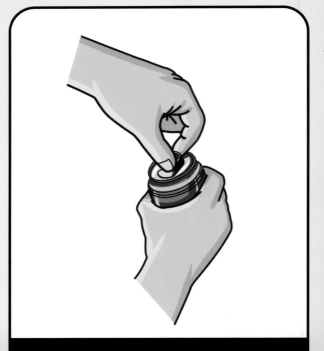

Effort: Fingers pulling up
Fulcrum: Where tab is attached to can
Load: Making drinking hole in can

Load: Lid of bottle

Fulcrum: Edge of bottle

Effort: Hand pulling up

Load: Fish

Fulcrum: Wrist or elbow

Effort: Hand

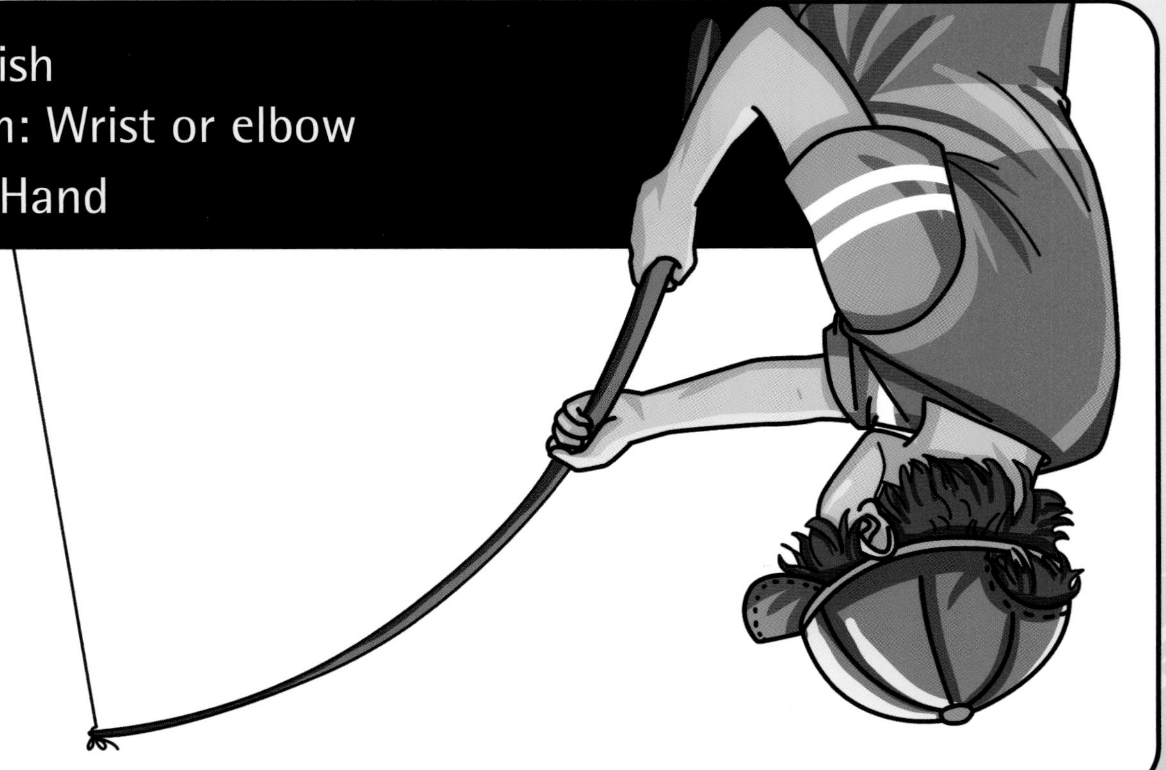

Working Together

You can accomplish more work by combining simple machines. A **complex machine** is two or more simple machines working together. Complex machines often use levers.

Many kinds of large construction equipment, such as backhoes and bulldozers, use levers and other simple machines.

Can you identify which of these tools are complex machines?

The arm for the scoop is a lever.

This excavator combines levers and other simple machines to move large loads of dirt. Digging with a simple shovel would be much more difficult.

Glossary

catapult A device used for throwing objects

complex machine A machine where two or more simple machines work together

effort The push or pull used to move an object

energy The ability to do work

first-class lever A lever with the fulcrum between the load and effort; helps lift large objects

fulcrum The fixed point around which a lever bar moves

lever A stiff bar that moves around a fixed spot

load The object to be moved

mechanical advantage How much easier and faster a machine makes work

second–class lever A lever with the load between the fulcrum and effort; helps lift large objects

third–class lever A lever with the effort between the load and fulcrum; helps move objects a long distance

work When a push or pull moves an object

Index

Web Sites

http://www.edheads.org/activities/simple-machines/

http://www.enchantedlearning.com/physics/machines/Levers.shtm

http://www.elizrosshubbell.com/levertutorial/index.html

Printed in the U.S.A. — CG